FIND FREDDIE AROUND THE WORLD

By
Anthony Tallarico

Incorporated

Copyright © 1992 Kidsbooks Inc. and Anthony Tallarico
7004 N. California Ave.
Chicago, IL 60645

Freddie has won an around the world vacation…and you're invited to come along! Stay close to Freddie, or you might get lost!

FIND FREDDIE IN THE UNITED STATES AND…

☐ Balloons (2)
☐ Barn
☐ Brooms (2)
☐ Buffalo
☐ Cactus (4)
☐ Campfire
☐ Cannon
☐ Cows (2)
☐ Coyote
☐ Footballs (2)
☐ Ghost
☐ Goat
☐ Guitars (2)
☐ Hockey player
☐ Jack-o'-lantern
☐ Kite
☐ Lighthouse
☐ Log cabin
☐ Moose
☐ Owl
☐ Periscope
☐ Scarecrows (2)
☐ Star
☐ Statue of Liberty
☐ Surfer
☐ Turtle
☐ Witch

Where did the elephant escape from?
Who is sleeping?
Where is Cuba?
What's on sale?
Where's the big cheese?

Freddie is northward bound as he travels to Canada, Alaska, Greenland, and Iceland.

FIND FREDDIE IN THIS WINTER WONDERLAND AND…

☐ Automobile
☐ Banana peel
☐ Bear
☐ Beaver
☐ Birds (2)
☐ Bone
☐ Box
☐ Bucket
☐ Elephant
☐ Elf
☐ Horse
☐ Ice-cream cone
☐ Igloo
☐ Jackrabbit
☐ Jester
☐ King Kong
☐ Lumberjack
☐ Mounty
☐ Oil well
☐ Pencil
☐ Pumpkin
☐ Scarecrow
☐ Seal
☐ Sleds (2)
☐ Snow castle
☐ Snowmen (2)
☐ Stars (2)
☐ Top hat
☐ Totem pole
☐ Unicycles

What's on sale? (3)
Where did Freddie take French lessons?
What's the 49th state?
Where's Greenland?
What's the capital of Canada?
Where's Nova Scotia?

Freddie heads southeast to the next three stops on his world tour: Ireland, Scotland, and England.

FIND FREDDIE IN THE BRITISH ISLES AND…

☐ Airplane
☐ Bagpiper
☐ Boats (7)
☐ Book
☐ Broom
☐ Bus
☐ Chicken
☐ Crown
☐ Dog
☐ Fish (8)
☐ Four-leaf
   clovers (4)
☐ Guitar
☐ Harp
☐ Horseshoe
☐ Kite
☐ Knight
☐ Magnifying glass
☐ Periscope
☐ Pig
☐ Pot of gold
☐ Sheep (3)
☐ Spear
☐ Stonehenge
☐ Telescope
☐ Turtle
☐ Umbrella

What games are they playing? (4)
What's for sale? (2)
Where's France?
Who did Freddie visit in Ireland?

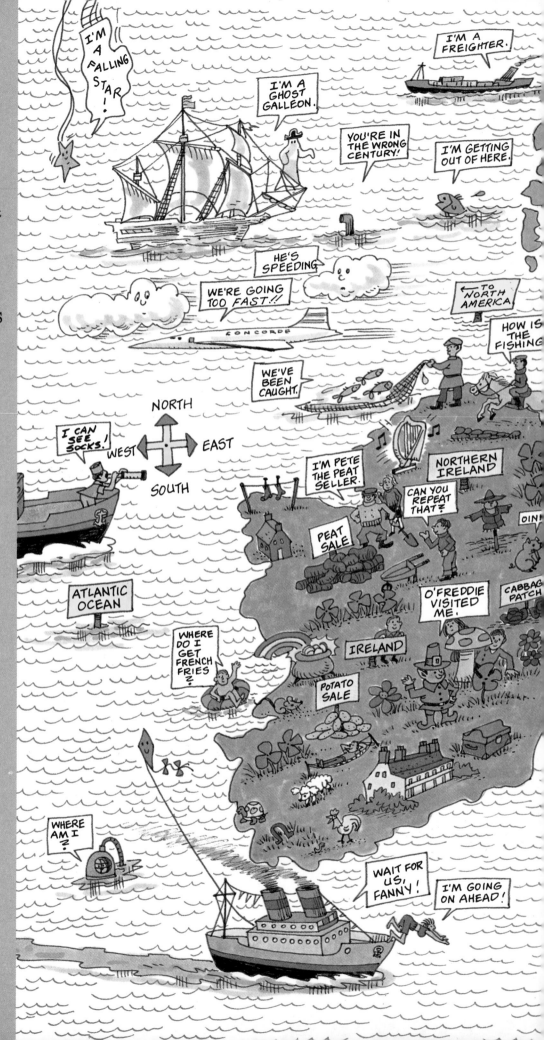

Freddie travels on throughout Europe...and you go along with him!

FIND FREDDIE AMONG THESE FRIENDLY FOREIGNERS AND...

- ☐ Artist
- ☐ Bather
- ☐ Beachball
- ☐ Bone
- ☐ Bull
- ☐ Camel
- ☐ Castle
- ☐ Dogs (2)
- ☐ Envelope
- ☐ Fire hydrant
- ☐ Heart
- ☐ Jack-o´-lantern
- ☐ Key
- ☐ Laundry
- ☐ Lost and Found
- ☐ Motorcycle
- ☐ Mountain goat
- ☐ Pencil
- ☐ Rabbit
- ☐ Sailboats (2)
- ☐ Santa Claus
- ☐ Skier
- ☐ Snowmen (2)
- ☐ Stars (2)
- ☐ Stork
- ☐ Tulip
- ☐ Turtles (2)
- ☐ Volcano
- ☐ Witch

Who was forgotten?
What gets wet?
Where do pandas live?
Where's the
   Strait of Gibraltar?

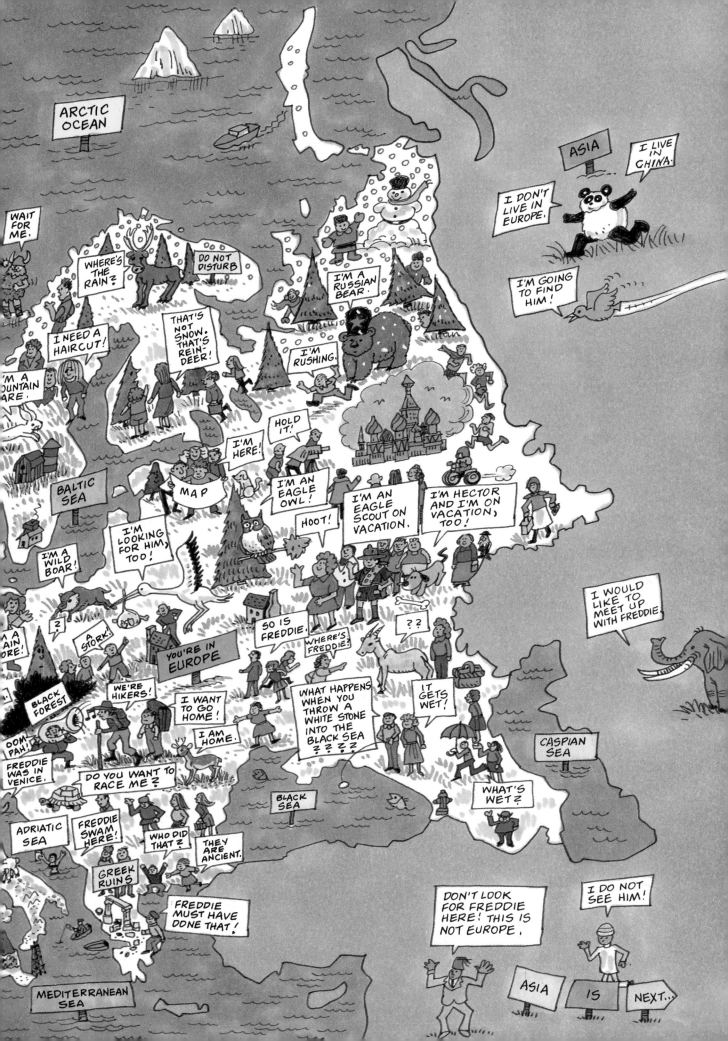

Next, Freddie is off to explore the largest continent, Asia. There are many things here that he's always wanted to see.

FIND FREDDIE IN THIS VAST AND EXOTIC LAND AND...

☐ Accordian player
☐ Balloon
☐ Bears (2)
☐ Birdcage
☐ Candy cane
☐ Chef
☐ Dragons (2)
☐ Fan
☐ Flying carpet
☐ Genie
☐ Heart
☐ Horse
☐ Kite
☐ Lemming
☐ Nutmeg tree
☐ Pandas (3)
☐ Peacock
☐ Reindeer
☐ Rice field
☐ Snakes (2)
☐ Surfer
☐ Tea cup
☐ Tears
☐ Telescope
☐ Tigers (2)
☐ Tire
☐ Turtle
☐ Water buffalo
☐ Yak

Where is the highest place on earth?
Which way is the North Pole?
Where's Japan?
Who needs the oasis?

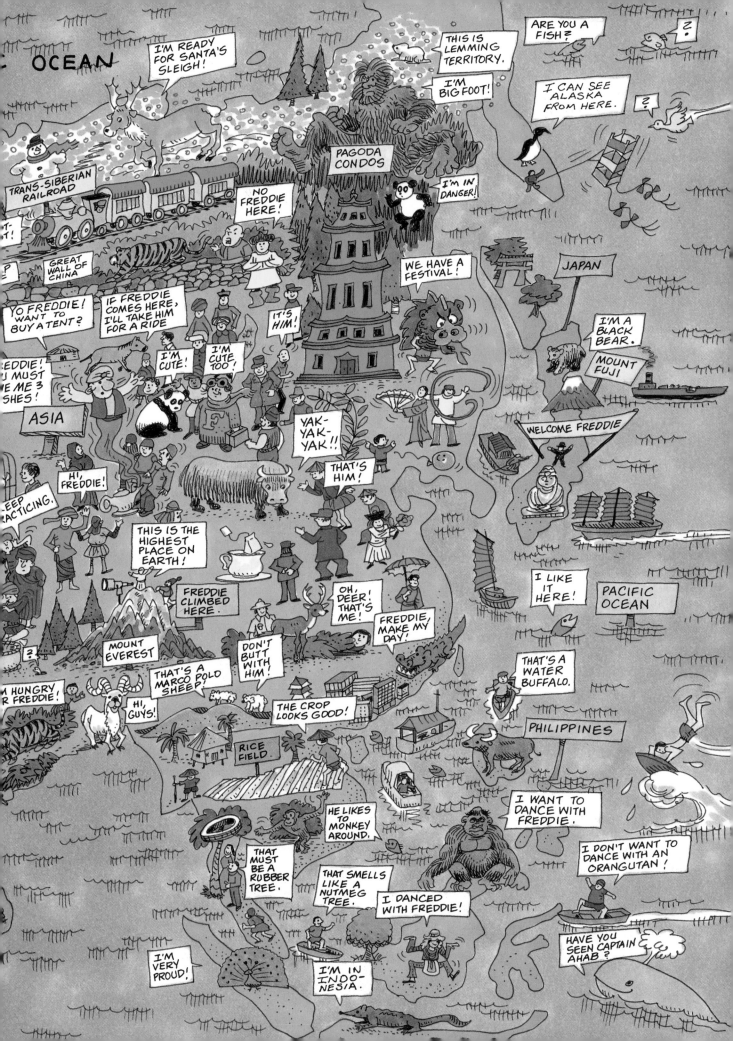

Freddie's next stop is a continent filled with amazing animals. I hope he doesn't get into any trouble there.

FIND FREDDIE IN THIS AFRICAN ADVENTURE-LAND AND...

- ☐ Aardvark
- ☐ Automobile
- ☐ Book
- ☐ Boot
- ☐ Bottle
- ☐ Camels (2)
- ☐ Cape buffalo
- ☐ Cape seal
- ☐ Crocodile
- ☐ Cup
- ☐ Date palm
- ☐ Drum
- ☐ Giraffes (2)
- ☐ Gnu
- ☐ Gorilla
- ☐ Heart
- ☐ Huts (4)
- ☐ Ibis
- ☐ Leopard
- ☐ Light bulb
- ☐ Monkeys (3)
- ☐ Ostrich
- ☐ Pelican
- ☐ Penguin
- ☐ Porcupine
- ☐ Rhino
- ☐ Snakes (3)
- ☐ Sunglasses (4)
- ☐ Top hat
- ☐ TV antennas (2)
- ☐ Umbrella

Who's the king of the jungle?
Who's wearing stripes?
Where's the Suez Canal?

Freddie arrives in Australia and takes a very interesting ride. He'll stop off in New Zealand, New Guinea, and Tasmania, too.

FIND FREDDIE IN THE LAND DOWN UNDER AND…

- ☐ Barbell
- ☐ Baseball bat
- ☐ Book
- ☐ Boomerang
- ☐ Chef
- ☐ Crane
- ☐ Dingo
- ☐ Dragon
- ☐ Fishermen (2)
- ☐ Football
- ☐ Ghost
- ☐ Golfer
- ☐ Horse
- ☐ Jogger
- ☐ Kite
- ☐ Koalas (3)
- ☐ Lost shorts
- ☐ Lost sock
- ☐ Lyrebird
- ☐ Paper airplane
- ☐ Rabbits (4)
- ☐ Scuba diver
- ☐ Shark fins (5)
- ☐ Sheep (4)
- ☐ Skateboard
- ☐ Stars (3)
- ☐ Tennis players (4)
- ☐ Tent
- ☐ Tire
- ☐ Tree kangaroo
- ☐ Umbrella
- ☐ Wombat

Which three birds can't fly?
What's on sale?
Where's the Great Barrier Reef?

Freddie's next stop is the continent that surrounds the South Pole—Antarctica! It's the coldest place in the world. Is Freddie dressed for it?

FIND FREDDIE IN THIS BLISTERY BLIZZARD AND...

☐ Artist
☐ Balloon
☐ Beachball
☐ Bottle
☐ Camel
☐ Chair
☐ Chef
☐ Earmuffs
☐ Fish (2)
☐ Icebergs (4)
☐ Jester
☐ Key
☐ Lost boot
☐ Lost mitten
☐ Magnifying glass
☐ Mailbox
☐ Palm tree
☐ Penguins (10)
☐ Pick
☐ Refrigerator
☐ Seals (4)
☐ Shovel
☐ Skaters (3)
☐ Snowmen (2)
☐ South Pole
☐ Surfboard
☐ Telescope
☐ Tents (4)
☐ Tire
☐ Whales (4)

What two things
  are for sale?
Who's from
  another planet?

Watch out fourth largest continent, Freddie is coming to visit!

FIND FREDDIE IN SOUTH AMERICA AND…

- [ ] Alpaca
- [ ] Anteater
- [ ] Bear
- [ ] Binoculars
- [ ] Bone
- [ ] Bus
- [ ] Cactus
- [ ] Coffee pot
- [ ] Cowboy
- [ ] Flamingos (2)
- [ ] Flying bats (2)
- [ ] Guitar
- [ ] Hammock
- [ ] Jeep
- [ ] Monkeys (3)
- [ ] Motorcyle
- [ ] Orchid
- [ ] Periscope
- [ ] Pineapple
- [ ] Rain slicker
- [ ] Santa Claus
- [ ] Snakes (4)
- [ ] Swamp deer
- [ ] Tires (2)
- [ ] Toucans (2)
- [ ] Tree frog
- [ ] Turtles (2)
- [ ] TV antenna
- [ ] Umbrellas (2)
- [ ] Wagon

What is the longest mountain range in the world?
What's a three-sided nut?

Freddie extends his stay in South America and then heads north to Central America.

FIND FREDDIE IN BETWEEN NORTH AND SOUTH AMERICA AND...

☐ Aliens (2)
☐ Balloons (2)
☐ Banana boat
☐ Bathtub
☐ Bullfighter
☐ Butterfly
☐ Candle
☐ Flamingo
☐ Frog
☐ Iron
☐ Jogger
☐ Oil well
☐ Paper airplane
☐ Periscope
☐ Pirate
☐ Pot
☐ Roller skates
☐ Rowboat
☐ Sailboats (4)
☐ Shark fin
☐ Sled
☐ Snowman
☐ Straw
☐ Super hero
☐ Surfer
☐ Sword
☐ Traffic cop
☐ Truck
☐ Water-skier

Which is the largest country in Central America?
What two countries share the same island?
What's for sale? (2)
What country is separated by a canal?

It looks like some aliens have been following Freddie on his trip. Maybe they're planning to take him home with them.

FIND FREDDIE ON HIS LAST STOP AND...

☐ Alarm clock
☐ Basketball net
☐ Bathtub
☐ Bowling ball
☐ Castle
☐ Chair
☐ Firecracker
☐ Fish (8)
☐ Flamingo
☐ Giraffe
☐ Hot dog
☐ Igloo
☐ Jack-in-the-box
☐ Jack-o´-lantern
☐ Jackrabbit
☐ Kite
☐ Knight
☐ Lost ice skate
☐ Moose
☐ Owl
☐ Pencil
☐ Shark fins (2)
☐ Shipwrecked sailor
☐ Skier
☐ Sleds (2)
☐ Snowman
☐ Surfer
☐ Tepee
☐ Turtle
☐ TV antennas (3)
☐ Umbrella
☐ Walrus

Where has the walrus never been?
What country is Siberia next to?

Freddie has finally come home. All his "Where Are They?" friends are happy to see him!

FIND FREDDIE AND...

☐ Baseball cap
☐ Book
☐ Candy cane
☐ Cheese
☐ Dish
☐ Feather
☐ Fork
☐ Four-leaf clover
☐ Hearts (2)
☐ Letter
☐ Lost sock
☐ Pig
☐ Rug
☐ Slipper
☐ Star

What's for sale?
Who missed
  Freddie the most?

FIND FREDDIE
AROUND THE WORL